Presidents of the United States Bio-Graphics

Bill Clinton

42nd U.S. President

Written by Joeming Dunn Illustrated by Ben Dunn

magic wagon

visit us at www.abdopublishing.com

Published by Magic Wagon, a division of the ABDO Publishing Group, 8000 West 78th Street, Edina, Minnesota 55439.

Printed in the United States of America, North Mankato, Minnesota.
042011
092011
This book contains at least 10% recycled materials.

Written by Joeming Dunn
Illustrated by Ben Dunn
Colored by Robby Bevard
Lettered by Doug Dlin
Edited by Stephanie Hedlund and Rochelle Baltzer
Interior layout and design by Antarctic Press
Cover art by Ben Dunn
Cover design by Abbey Fitzgerald

Library of Congress Cataloging-in-Publication Data

Dunn, Joeming W.
Bill Clinton : 42nd U.S. president / written by Joeming Dunn ; illustrated by Ben Dunn.
p. cm. -- (Presidents of the United States bio-graphics)
Includes index.
ISBN 978-1-61641-645-4
1. Clinton, Bill, 1946---Juvenile literature. 2. Presidents--United States--Biography--Juvenile literature. 3. Clinton, Bill, 1946---Comic books, strips, etc. 4. Presidents--United States--Biography--Comic books, strips, etc. 5. Graphic novels. I. Dunn, Ben, ill. II. Title.
E886.D86 2012
973.929092--dc22
[B]

2011010672

Table of Contents

I DO SOLEMNLY SWEAR (OR AFFIRM) THAT I WILL FAITHFULLY EXECUTE THE OFFICE OF PRESIDENT OF THE UNITED STATES, AND WILL TO THE BEST OF MY ABILITY, PRESERVE, PROTECT AND DEFEND THE CONSTITUTION OF THE UNITED STATES.

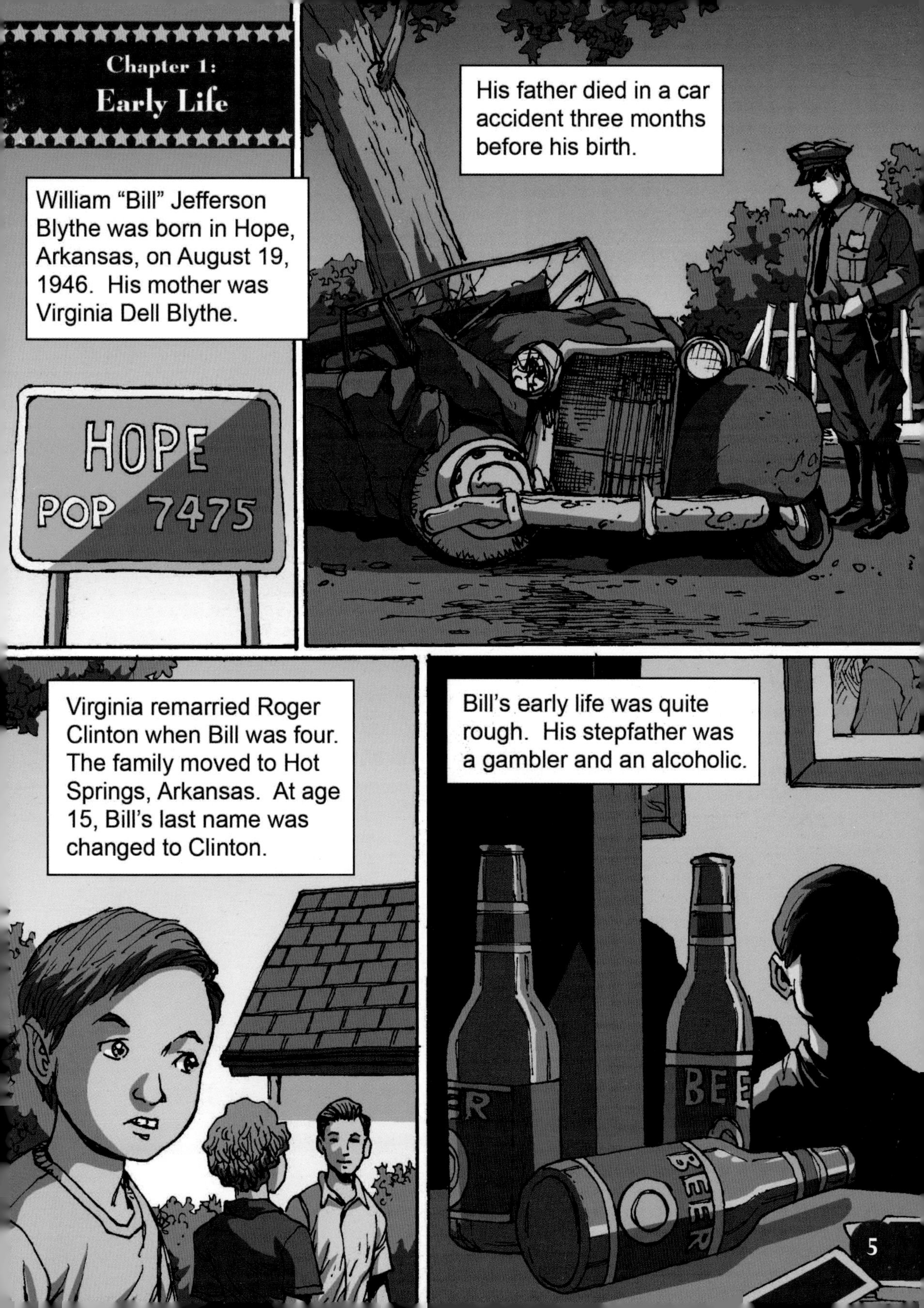
Chapter 1:
Early Life
William "Bill" Jefferson Blythe was born in Hope, Arkansas, on August 19, 1946. His mother was Virginia Dell Blythe.
HOPE
POP 7475
His father died in a car accident three months before his birth.
Virginia remarried Roger Clinton when Bill was four. The family moved to Hot Springs, Arkansas. At age 15, Bill's last name was changed to Clinton.
Bill's early life was quite rough. His stepfather was a gambler and an alcoholic.
ER
BEE
BEER

Despite this, Bill did well in school and in band.
At age 17, Bill got to learn firsthand about the electoral process. He visited Washington DC and met with then-president John F. Kennedy.
After high school, Bill went to Georgetown University in Washington DC. He graduated in 1968 with a degree in International Studies.
Georgetown University
While at Georgetown, he worked as an intern for Senator William Fulbright of Arkansas.

During this time, the United States was involved in the Vietnam War.
Many were against the war, including Clinton.
OUT OF
NO
After graduation, Clinton attended the University of Oxford in England. Because of this, he was able to stay out of the Vietnam War.

Chapter 2: Running for Office

In 1978, Clinton ran for governor of Arkansas.
CLINTON
for
He beat Republican Lynn Lowe. Clinton became one of the youngest governors ever elected.
One of the first things Clinton did as governor was try to improve the state's highways and roads.
To do this, he added a state tax on gasoline and automobiles.
ROAD WORK AHEAD

The new tax was not popular. Clinton was voted out of office in 1980. But, he was reelected as governor in 1982.
Clinton felt that education was very important. He appointed his wife as head of the Education Commission.
SCHOOL
Some of the changes that were made included requiring testing for teachers and students and increasing pay for teachers.
Clinton also gave tax breaks to many companies to encourage investment in the state.

Clinton's popularity grew. In 1988, he was asked to give a speech for Massachusetts governor Michael Dukakis at the Democratic National Convention.
Dukakis later lost to then-vice president George H.W. Bush.
Now Clinton was thrust into the national spotlight.
He was involved in the Democratic Leadership Council, the Southern Growth Policies, and the National Governor's Association.
In 1990, Saddam Hussein sent Iraqi soldiers to invade the neighboring country of Kuwait.
Many countries didn't approve of Iraq's actions. The United States joined forces with them to form Operation Desert Storm. It successfully drove Iraqi forces from Kuwait in 1991.

Chapter 3:
Campaigning for President
Due to the success of the operation, many believed President Bush would be reelected. Many Democrats chose not to run.
That did not stop Clinton from announcing his candidacy for president.
BILL Clinton FOR PRESIDENT
The road to the White House was rough. Clinton was ranked behind Senators Tom Harking and Paul Tsongas.
At the start of the primaries, Clinton finished a distant third.

Within weeks, a scandal hit the Clinton campaign.
CLINTON SCANDAL!
The Clintons appeared on *60 Minutes* to deny the affair.
The interview was a great success. Clinton finished a strong second to Paul Tsongas in New Hampshire.
After the close victory, Clinton labeled himself the Comeback Kid.

Clinton then easily captured many of the southern states. This led him to get the Democratic presidential nomination.
He selected Tennessee senator Al Gore as his running mate.
This was a somewhat risky choice, since both came from southern states.
Clinton would face two challengers, George H.W. Bush and Ross Perot.

His opponents immediately went on the attack. They argued that Clinton would raise taxes and that he did not have enough experience in foreign policy.
Form 1040
Label
(See instructions on page 16.)
Use the IRS label.
LABEL
Clinton took a grassroots approach to the election.
He painted himself as a person of the people.
He traveled around the country and met people.
TOWN HALL MEETING
Clinton also made himself easily available to the media. He appeared on talk and news shows.

He even played the saxophone on a late night TV program.

PLEASE HELP
Bush was popular after Operation Desert Storm. But, the economy was not doing well, and he had broken his promise of "no new taxes."

Clinton easily won the election of 1992. He became the 42nd president of the United States on January 20, 1993.
THERE IS NOTHING WRONG WITH AMERICA THAT CANNOT BE CURED BY WHAT IS RIGHT WITH AMERICA.
SEAL OF THE PRESIDENT OF THE UNITED STATES